Graphs in Action

Graphing

Andrew Einspruch

Publishing Credits

Editor
Sara Johnson

Editorial Director
Dona Herweck Rice

Editor-in-Chief
Sharon Coan, M.S.Ed.

Creative Director
Lee Aucoin

Publisher
Rachelle Cracchiolo, M.S.Ed.

Image Credits

The author and publisher would like to gratefully credit or acknowledge the following for permission to reproduce copyright material: The author and publisher would like to gratefully credit or acknowledge the following for permission to reproduce copyright material: cover Shutterstock; p.1 Photolibrary.com / Alamy; p.4 Shutterstock; pp.6–8 Shutterstock; p.10 iStock Photos; pp.12–13 Shutterstock; p.15 Photolibrary.com; p.17 Photolibrary.com/Alamy; p.19 Photolibrary.com; p.22 Shutterstock; p. 24 Shutterstock; p. 26 Big Stock Photo; p.27 Shutterstock

While every care has been taken to trace and acknowledge copyright, the publishers tender their apologies for any accidental infringement where copyright has proved untraceable. They would be pleased to come to a suitable arrangement with the rightful owner in each case.

Teacher Created Materials

5301 Oceanus Drive
Huntington Beach, CA 92649-1030
http://www.tcmpub.com

ISBN 978-0-7439-0923-5

Table of Contents

Showing Information

Graphs are a kind of picture. They show **data**, usually numbers, **visually** (VIZ-you-uh-lee). Graphs are good for comparing data. They must be **accurate**. And they need to have clear labels and titles. The graphs on these pages show information about a small ice cream business.

Bar Graphs

A bar graph shows data for different groups. This bar graph **compares** the number of ice cream sundaes sold each month during one year.

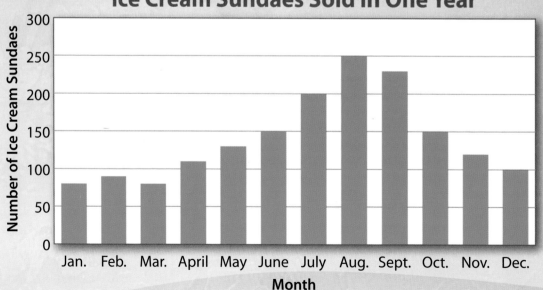

Ice Cream Sundaes Sold in One Year

Circle Graphs

A circle graph is useful to show how parts of data relate to the whole. This circle graph compares the sales of different flavors of ice cream. The circle graph shows all the ice creams sold. Each part of the circle shows a different flavor. The **key** tells us which color **represents** each flavor.

Ice Cream Flavors Sold

Key
- ■ Chocolate
- ■ Strawberry
- ■ Vanilla
- ⁙ Cookies and Cream
- ■ Peppermint

LET'S EXPLORE MATH

Use the bar graph on page 4 to answer these questions.

a. Which 3 months had the highest ice cream sales?

b. What was the total number of ice cream sundaes sold in the months of June and October?

Use the circle graph above to answer these questions.

c. Which flavor is the least popular?

d. Which flavor is more popular, strawberry or vanilla?

Often, data in tables can be turned into graphs. This table shows data from a small clothing business. It shows how many different **items** of clothing were sold during the month of July.

Clothing Sold in July

Clothing Items	Baseball caps	Jackets	Pants	Shirts	Sweaters
Number of Items Sold	35	20	15	25	5

A bar graph can be made using the data in the table. This bar graph makes it easy to compare the sales numbers quickly.

The information in the table can also be shown in a circle graph. But the exact number of each item sold is not shown. Instead, this circle graph shows **percents**. The whole circle graph stands for 100 percent (%). Each part of the circle stands for part of that 100 percent (%).

Clothing Sold in July

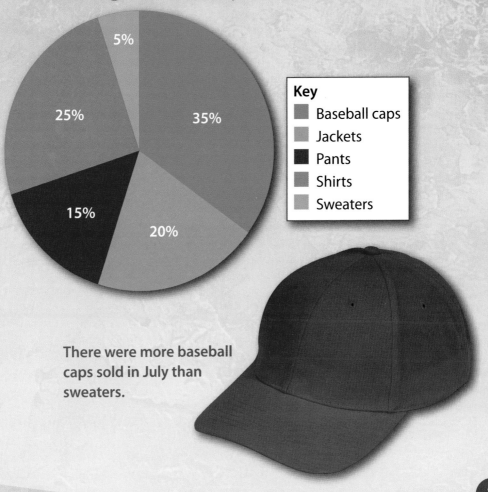

Key
- Baseball caps
- Jackets
- Pants
- Shirts
- Sweaters

There were more baseball caps sold in July than sweaters.

Line Graphs

Line graphs are a good way to show data **continuously** collected over time. It could be data that has been collected every day for a week, month, or year. The temperature information in this table was collected daily for a week.

Mount Baw Baw Daily Maximum Temperature

Day of the Week	Daily Maximum Temperature
Monday	29°F (-1.7°C)
Tuesday	34°F (1.1°C)
Wednesday	39°F (3.9°C)
Thursday	30°F (-1.1°C)
Friday	40°F (4.4°C)
Saturday	42°F (5.6°C)
Sunday	30°F (-1.1°C)

Mount Baw Baw is a mountain in Victoria, Australia. Its name is said to be an Australian Aboriginal term for "echo."

A line graph can be made using the data in the table. A point on the graph shows the highest temperature reached each day. A line connects the points. This makes it easy to see how the temperature changes during the week.

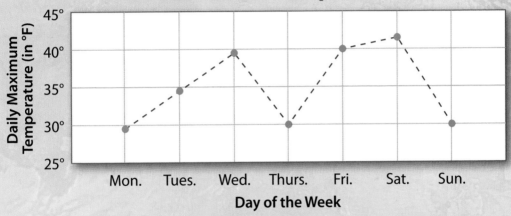

Mount Baw Baw Daily Maximum Temperature

Does It Have an Axis?

Many different kinds of graphs have an *x*-axis and a *y*-axis. The *x*-axis is the horizontal line of the graph. The *y*-axis is the vertical line. Each axis has a label. Which type of graph does not have an *x*- and a *y*-axis?

This table shows data collected over a period of time. The data gives the population of Acorn Town. The data was collected every 100 years from 1700 to 2000.

Acorn Town Population

Year	Population
1700	20,000
1800	50,000
1900	65,000
2000	55,000

It is important to choose the right graph to show information. A bar graph is a great way to show big differences in data. Compare the population of Acorn Town for the years 1700 and 1900 in this graph.

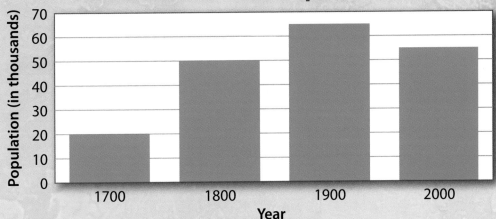

Acorn Town Population

LET'S EXPLORE MATH

This table shows the population growth of Thatcham, a small town in England. Create a bar graph using this data. *Hint*: Label the *x*- and *y*-axis and give your graph a title.

Year	1991	2001	2005
Approximate Population	15,000	21,000	23,000

Making Graphs Clear

It is important that information on a graph is clear. This **pictograph** uses pictures of dogs. Each picture represents the number of dogs living in 3 different cities in Central County. The pictures of dogs look good, but the information on the graph is not clear. It looks as if each city has only one breed of dog living there. The graph has a title but no x- or y-axis labels. The different kinds of dogs are also **distracting** and keep the reader from finding out the correct information.

Dogs Living in Central County Cities

Left Town   Centralville   Right City

The pictograph below shows the same information about the number of dogs living in Central County. But it uses the same picture to show the information for each city. It also uses a key to explain what the picture means. What does this graph tell you?

Dogs Living in Central County Cities

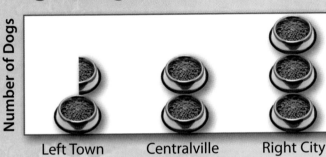

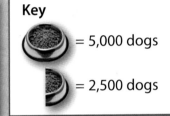

Key

= 5,000 dogs

= 2,500 dogs

Left Town   Centralville   Right City

Cities

Number of Dogs

LET'S EXPLORE MATH

Use the pictograph above to answer these questions.

a. How many dogs live in Left Town?

b. How many more dogs live in Right City than in Centralville?

c. How many dogs in total live in the 3 Central County cities?

d. If you were setting up a dog-washing business, which city would you live in? Give reasons for your answer.

Graphs need to be clear so we can understand the information they show. If they are not clear, they are not useful. Look at this bar graph. What information does it tell you? Is it useful?

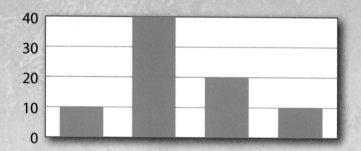

Now look at the same graph with a label on each axis.

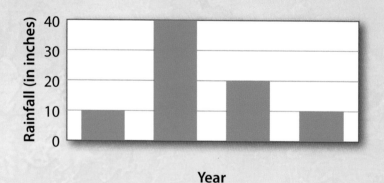

Now we know that the graph is showing rainfall over time. But we still need more information for the graph to make sense and be useful.

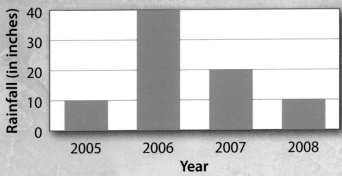

Rainfall in Lake Town

The *x*-axis shows that we are looking at rainfall for the years 2005 to 2008. The *y*-axis shows the amount of rainfall measured in inches. The title tells us what the graph is about.

Lake Town is represented in the graph above.

The type of bar graph below is called a double bar graph. It allows you to compare 2 sets of data on 1 graph. The key tells us that the colored bars represent 2 different towns. It is easy to see what is the same and what is different about the rainfall in each town.

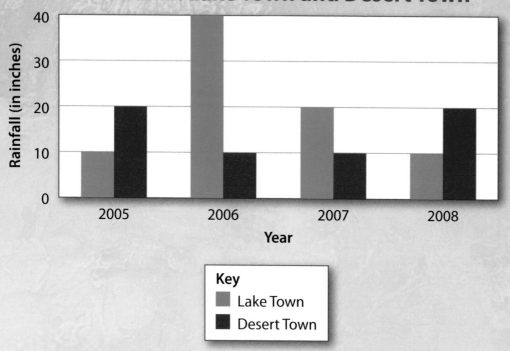

Rainfall in Lake Town and Desert Town

Key
Lake Town
Desert Town

The double bar graph shows that Lake Town received more rain during the years 2006 and 2007 than Desert Town. But it also shows that in 2005 and 2008, Desert Town received 10 inches more rain than Lake Town.

LET'S EXPLORE MATH

Use the double bar graph on page 16 to answer these questions.

a. Figure out the total amount of rain each town received over the 4-year time span.

b. Which town had the greater rainfall overall?

c. How much more rain did Lake Town receive in 2006 than Desert Town?

d. Which town would you rather live in? Why?

Desert Town has a very dry climate.

Graphs in Business

Business owners find graphs very useful. Graphs can show how sales, and other things, change over time. They can also help us see what might happen in the future.

The owners of Best's Grocery Store use graphs to show sales information. The products they sell are put into **categories**. This bar graph shows the amount of products sold last year.

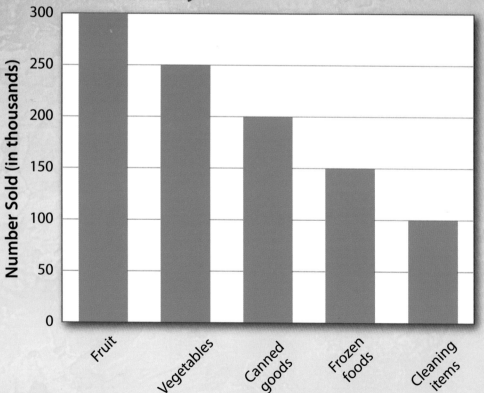

Best's Grocery Store Products Sold in 2008

Another way to show the amount of products sold last year is to use a circle graph. The colored sections make it easy to compare how big or small the amounts are in relation to the total number of products sold.

In this circle graph, the section for fruit is the biggest. This means the store sells more fruit than any other product. The section for cleaning items is the smallest. And the amounts for vegetables and canned goods are about the same. The owners can see this information without needing to know exact numbers.

Best's Grocery Store Products Sold in 2008

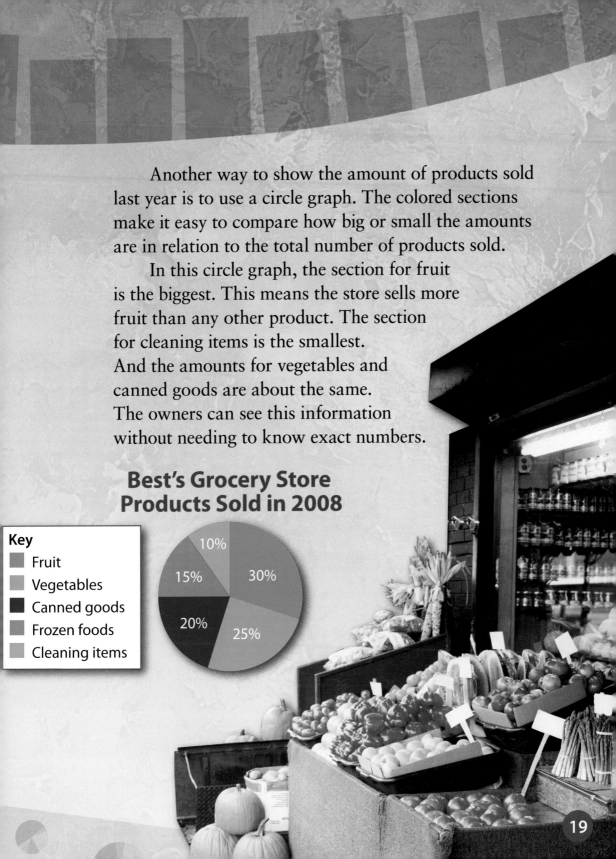

Key
- Fruit
- Vegetables
- Canned goods
- Frozen foods
- Cleaning items

10%
15%
30%
20%
25%

Businesses also use graphs to find out how much they are selling and when. This line graph shows the amount of sales at Best's Grocery Store for each month of 2008.

Best's Grocery Store Sales in 2008

Graphs are a good way of showing what is happening in a business. The line graph shows that the sales at the store are growing. Not every month has more sales than the month before, but the **trend** is upward.

The owners also could use a bar graph to show the same information. Which do you think better shows the information, the line graph or the bar graph?

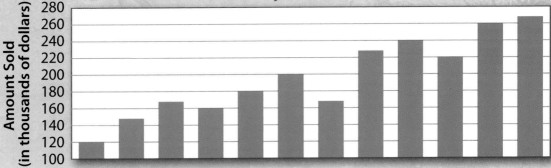

Best's Grocery Store Sales in 2008

LET'S EXPLORE MATH

Jackson sells new cars. This table shows how many new cars he sold in the first 6 months of the year.

Jan.	Feb.	Mar.	Apr.	May	June
25	28	32	30	34	35

a. Create a bar graph using this data. Then create a line graph of the same data.

b. Write a sales report telling what trend you can see in the sales.

The owners of Best's Grocery Store are interested in seeing the sales this year, but they also want to know how the sales compare with last year. This line graph shows last year's sales information.

Best's Grocery Store Sales in 2007

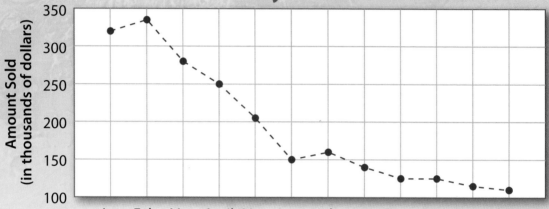

This line graph shows this year's sales information.

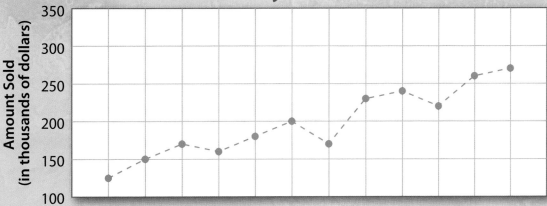

Best's Grocery Store Sales in 2008

What do the graphs show about the business? The owners can see that sales dropped during 2007, and rose again in 2008. However, by the end of 2008, sales were still not as good as they were in early 2007.

Why did sales drop in 2007? Did a new store open in the neighborhood? Why did sales start to improve again in 2008? Graphs can help the owners ask questions and make decisions about their businesses.

Graphs Working Together

Different kinds of graphs can be used together to provide information. A business might want to find out about visitors to its website. Graphs can show this information in different ways.

This bar graph below shows the number of visitors to the website over a 6-month period.

Visitors to Website over 6 Months

Number of Visitors (in Thousands)

Month

This circle graph shows how many people visited the website for the first time. It also shows how many people have visited before.

Visitors to Website

Key ▓ New visitors
■ Previous visitors

How Website Was Found

This circle graph shows how visitors got to the website. Some used **search engines** and some came from other websites.

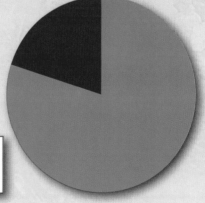

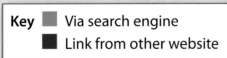

Key ▓ Via search engine
■ Link from other website

Each graph shows different information. Together they help to build a complete picture of who visits the website.

Graphs Around You

Readers of newspapers and magazines sometimes look at pictures before words. So, newspapers and magazines make graphs that grab the readers' attention. This circle graph has sections of the circle standing out.

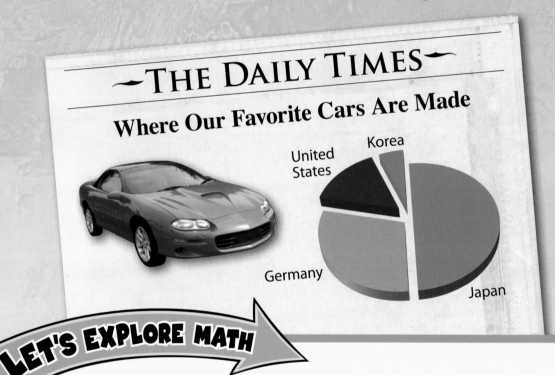

~THE DAILY TIMES~

Where Our Favorite Cars Are Made

United States

Korea

Germany

Japan

LET'S EXPLORE MATH

Look at the circle graph above.

a. Which country makes the greatest number of favorite cars?

b. Does the United States make more favorite cars than Germany?

c. Write a newspaper headline and article about the graph.

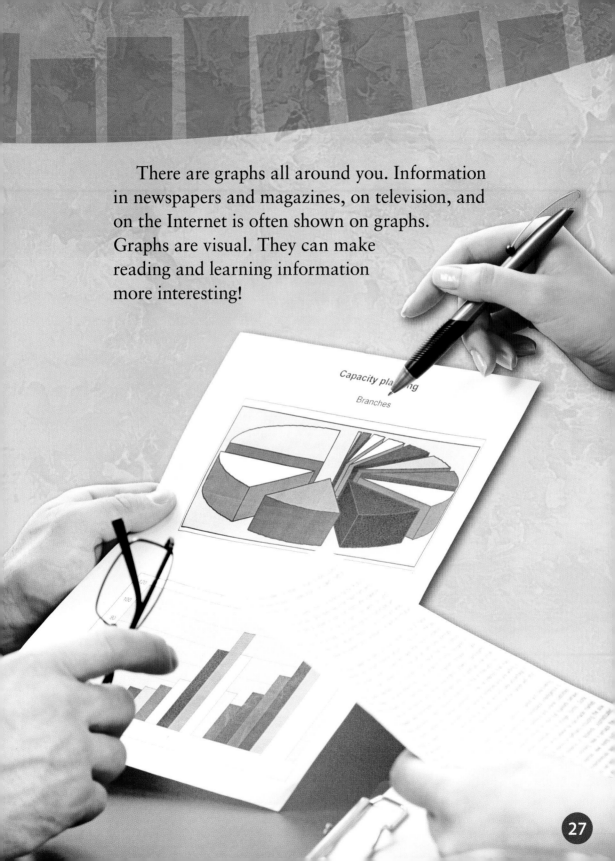

There are graphs all around you. Information in newspapers and magazines, on television, and on the Internet is often shown on graphs. Graphs are visual. They can make reading and learning information more interesting!

Capacity planning

Branches

Surf's Up?

Emilio owns a small surfing goods store. He would like to expand his business. The store next door is available to rent. Emilio needs to find out if his business is growing to see if he can afford to expand.

Business expenses total $1,200 per month for 2008. Emilio creates a circle graph to show the percentage of different expenses.

Breakdown of Expenses

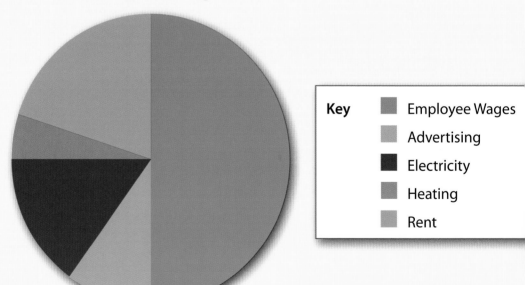

Key
- Employee Wages
- Advertising
- Electricity
- Heating
- Rent

Emilio also makes a table to show his sales per month for the past year.

2008 Sales

Jan.	Feb.	Mar.	Apr.	May	June
$900	$900	$1,100	$1,400	$1,500	$1,800

July	Aug.	Sept.	Oct.	Nov.	Dec.
$2,000	$2,100	$1,700	$1,500	$1,300	$1,300

Solve It!

Use the circle graph on page 28 to figure out:

a. Which expense costs Emilio the most each month?

b. Which expense costs Emilio the least each month?

Now use the table above to complete these questions.

c. Create a bar graph to show the sales for 2008.

d. Do you think Emilio should expand his business? List your reasons.

Use the steps below to help you create your graph. Remember to label the axes and give your graph a title.

Step 1: First, decide what data in the table to use for the *x*-axis and *y*-axis.

Step 2: Now create your bar graph using the amounts in the table. Label the graph and give it a title.

Glossary

accurate—correct

categories—groups containing items of a similar type

compares—looks at the features of two or more things to see how they are the same or different

continuously—nonstop; uninterrupted

data—information

distracting—related to something that interrupts thought or concentration

items—pieces

key—a list that explains symbols

percents—the rates or proportions per hundred

pictograph—a graph that uses pictures to represent information

represents—shows

search engines—computer programs that get information from a database or network

trend—a general direction in which something is heading

visually—as a picture, image, or display

Index

Let's Explore Math

Page 5:

a. July, August, September

b. 300 ice cream sundaes

c. Peppermint

d. Strawberry

Page 11:

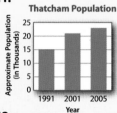

Page 13:

a. 7,500 dogs

b. 5,000 more dogs

c. 32,500 dogs

d. Answers will vary but should include Right City because the pictograph shows that it has the most dogs.

Page 17:

a. Lake Town received 80 inches of rain over the 4 years. Desert Town received 60 inches.

b. Lake Town

c. 30 more inches of rain

d. Answers will vary.

Page 21:

a.

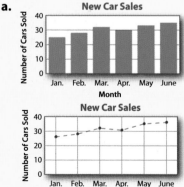

b. Answers may vary but could include the observation that sales continue to rise each month except for April where sales drop a little.

Page 26:

a. Japan

b. No, Germany makes more.

c. Answers will vary.

Problem-Solving Activity

a. Employee wages

b. Heating

c.

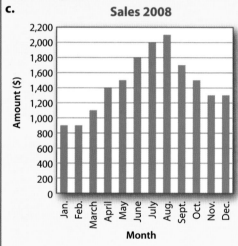

d. Answers may vary, but given that the bar graph shows that Emilio is making more sales and is meeting his expenses, he could afford to expand his business.